Life in the Southern States

Life in the Southern States

WHAT BECAME OF THE SLAVES ON A GEORGIA PLANTATION? GREAT AUCTION SALE OF SLAVES, AT SAVANNAH, GEORGIA,

MARCH 2d & 3d, 1859.

By

Price M. Butler

ISBN 978-1-105-15315-0

A SEQUEL TO MRS. KEMBLE's JOURNAL. Savannah, Ga. 1863.

SALE OF SLAVES.

The largest sale of human chattels that has been made in Star-Spangled America for several years, took place on Wednesday and Thursday of last week, at the Race-course near the City of Savannah, Georgia. The lot consisted of four hundred and thirty-six men, women, children and infants, being that half of the negro stock remaining on the old Major Butler plantations which fell to one of the two heirs to that estate. Major Butler, dying, left a property valued at more than a million of dollars, the major part of which was invested in rice and cotton plantations, and the slaves thereon, all of which immense fortune descended to two heirs, his sons, Mr. John A. Butler, sometime deceased, and Mr. Pierce M. Butler, still living, and resident in the City of Philadelphia, in the free State of Pennsylvania.

Losses in the great crash of 1857-8, and other exigencies of business, have compelled the latter gentleman to realize on his Southern investments, that he may satisfy his pressing creditors. This necessity led to a partition of the negro stock on the Georgia plantations, between himself and the representative of the other heir, the widow of the late John A. Butler, and the negroes that were brought to the hammer last week were the property of Mr. Pierce M. Butler, of Philadelphia, and were in fact sold to pay Mr. Pierce M. Butler's debts. The creditors were represented by Gen. Cadwalader, while Mr. Butler was present in person, attended by his business agent, to attend to his own interests.

The sale had been advertised largely for many weeks, though the name of Mr. Butler was not mentioned; and as the negroes were known to be a choice lot and very desirable property, the attendance of buyers was large. The breaking up of an old family estate is so uncommon an occurrence that the affair was regarded with unusual interest throughout the South. For several days before the sale every hotel in Savannah was crowded with negro speculators from North and South Carolina, Virginia, Georgia, Alabama, and

Louisiana, who had been attracted hither by the prospects of making good bargains. Nothing was heard for days, in the bar-rooms and public rooms, but talk of the great sale; criticisms of the business affairs of Mr. Butler, and speculations as to the probable prices the stock would bring. The office of Joseph Bryan, the Negro Broker, who had the management of the sale, was thronged every day by eager inquirers in search of information, and by some who were anxious to buy, but were uncertain as to whether their securities would prove acceptable.

Little parties were made up from the various hotels every day to visit the Race-course, distant some three miles from the city, to look over the chattels, discuss their points, and make memoranda for guidance on the day of sale. The buyers were generally of a rough breed, slangy, profane, and bearish, being for the most part from the back river and swamp plantations, where the elegancies of polite life are not, perhaps, developed to their fullest extent. In fact, the humanities are sadly neglected by the petty tyrants of the rice-fields that border the great Dismal Swamp, their knowledge of the luxuries of our best society comprehending only revolvers and kindred delicacies.

Your correspondent was present at an early date; but as he easily anticipated the touching welcome that would, at such a time, be officiously extended to a representative of *The Tribute*, and being a modest man withal, and not desiring to be the recipient of a public demonstration from the enthusiastic Southern population, who at times overdo their hospitality and their guests, he did not placard his mission and claim his honors. Although he kept his business in the back-ground, he made himself a prominent figure in the picture, and, wherever there was anything going on, there was he in the midst.

At the sale might have been seen a busy individual, armed with pencil and catalogue, doing his little utmost to keep up all the appearance of a knowing buyer, pricing "likely nigger fellers," talking confidentially to the smartest ebon maids, chucking the round-eyed youngsters under the chin, making an occasional bid for a large family, (a low bid--so low that somebody always instantly raised him twenty-five dollars, when the busy man would ignominiously retreat,) and otherwise conducting himself like a rich planter, with forty thousand dollars where he could put his finger on it. This gentleman was much condoled with by some sympathizing persons, when the particularly fine lot on which he had fixed his eye was sold and lost to him forever, because he happened to be down stairs at lunch just at the interesting moment.

WHERE THE NEGROES CAME FROM.

The negroes came from two plantations, the one a rice plantation near Darien, in the State of Georgia, not far from the great Okefonokee Swamp, and the other a cotton plantation on the extreme northern point of St. Simon's Island, a little bit of an island in the Atlantic, cut off from Georgia mainland by a slender arm of the sea. Though the most of the steek had been accustomed only to rice and cotton planting, there were among them a number of very passable mechanics, who had been taught to do all the rougher sorts of mechanical work on the plantations. There were coopers, carpenters, shoemakers and blacksmiths, each one equal, in his various craft, to the ordinary requirements of a plantation; thus, the coopers could make rice-tierces, and possibly, on a pinch, rude tubs and buckets; the carpenter could do the rough carpentry about the negro-quarters; the shoemaker could make shoes of the fashion required for the slaves, and the blacksmith was adequate to the manufacture of hoes and similar simple tools, and to such trifling repairs in the blacksmithing way as did not require too refined a skill. Though probably no one of all these would be called a superior, or even an average workman, among the masters of the craft, their knowledge of these various trades sold in some cases for nearly as much as the man--that is, a man without a trade, who would be valued at $900, would readily bring $1,600 or $1,700 if he was a passable blacksmith or cooper.

There were no light mulattoes in the whole lot of the Butler stock, and but very few that were even a shade removed from the original Congo blackness. They have been little defiled by the admixture of degenerate Anglo-Saxon blood, and, for the most part, could boast that they were of as pure a breed as the best blood of Spain--a point in their favor in the eyes of the buyer as well as physiologically, for too liberal an infusion of the blood of the dominant race brings a larger intelligence, a more vigorous brain, which, anon, grows restless under the yoke, and is prone to inquire into the definition of the word Liberty, and the meaning of the starry flag which waves, as you may have heard, o'er the land of the free. The pure-blooded negroes are much more docile and manageable than mulattoes, though less quick of comprehension, which makes them preferred by drivers, who can stimulate stupidity much easier than they can control intelligence by the lash.

None of the Butler slaves have ever been sold before, but have been on these two plantations since they were born. Here have they lived their humble lives, and loved their simple loves; here were they born, and here have many of them had children born unto them; here had their parents lived before them, and are now resting in quiet graves on the old plantations that these unhappy ones are to see no more forever; here they left not only the well-known scenes dear to them from very baby-hood by a thousand fond memories, and homes as much loved by them, perhaps, as brighter homes by men of brighter faces; but all the clinging ties that bound them to living hearts were torn asunder, for but one-half of each of these two happy little communities was sent to the shambles, to be scattered to the four winds, and the other half was left behind. And who can tell how closely intertwined are the affections of a little band of four hundred persons, living isolated from all the world beside, from birth to middle age? Do they not naturally become one great family, each man a brother unto each?

It is true they were sold "in families," but let us see: a man and his wife were called a "family," their parents and kindred were not taken into account; the man and wife might be sold to the pine woods of North Carolina, their brothers and sisters be scattered through the cotton fields of Alabama and rice swamps of Louisiana, while the parents might be left on the old plantation to wear out their weary lives in grief, and lay their heads in far-off graves, over which their children might never weep. And no account could be taken of loves that were as yet unconsummated by marriage; and how many aching hearts have been divorced by this summary proceeding no man can ever know. And the separation is as utter, and is infinitely more hopeless, than that made by the Angel of Death, for then the loved ones are committed to the care of a merciful Deity; but in the other instance, to the tender mercies of a slave-trade.

These dark-skinned unfortunates are perfectly unlettered, and could not communicate by writing even if they should know where to send their missives. And so to each other, and to the old familiar places of their youth, clung all their sympathies and affections, not less strong, perhaps, because they are so few. The blades of grass on all the Butler estates are outnumbered by the tears that are poured out in agony at the wreck that has been wrought in happy homes, and the crushing grief that has been laid on loving hearts.

But, then, what business have "niggers" with tears? Besides, didn't Pierce Butler give them a silver dollar a-piece? which will appear in the sequel. And, sad as it is, it was all necessary, because a gentleman was not able to live on the beggarly pittance of half a million, and so must needs enter into speculations which turned out adversely.

The negroes were brought to Savannah in small lots, as many at a time as could be conveniently taken care of, the last of them reaching the city the Friday before the sale. They were consigned to the care of Mr. J. Bryan, Auctioneer and Negro Broker, who was to feed and keep them in condition until disposed of. Immediately on their arrival they were taken to the Race-course, and there quartered in the sheds erected for the accommodation of the horses and carriages of gentlemen attending the races. Into these sheds they were huddled pell-mell, without any more attention to their comfort than was necessary to prevent their becoming ill and unsaleable. Each "family" had one or more boxes or bundles, in which were stowed such scanty articles of their clothing as were not brought into immediate requisition, and their tin dishes and gourds for their food and drink.

It is, perhaps, a fit tribute to large-handed munificence to say that, when the negro man was sold, there was no extra change for the negro man's clothes; they went with the man, and were not charged in the bill. Nor is this altogether a contemptible idea, for many of them had worldly wealth, in the shape of clothing and other valuables, to the extent of perhaps four or five dollars; and had all these been taken strictly into the account, the sum total of the sale would have been increased, possibly, a thousand dollars. In the North, we do not necessarily sell the harness with the horse; why, in the South, should the clothes go with the negro?

In these sheds were the chattels huddled together on the floor, there being no sign of bench or table. They eat and slept on the bare boards, their food being rice and beans, with occasionally a bit of bacon and corn bread. Their huge bundles were scattered over the floor, and thereon the slaves sat or reclined, when not restlessly moving about, or gathered into sorrowful groups, discussing the chances of their future fate.

On the faces of all was an expression of heavy grief; some appeared to be resigned to the hard stroke of Fortune that had torn them from their homes, and were sadly trying to make the best of it; some sat brooding moodily over their sorrows, their chins resting on their hands, their eyes staring vacantly, and their bodies rocking to and fro, with a restless motion that was never stilled; few wept, the place was too public and the drivers too near, though some occasionally turned aside to give way to a few quiet tears.

They were dressed in every possible variety of uncouth and fantastic garb, in every style and of every imaginable color; the texture of the garments was in all cases coarse, most of the men being clothed in the rough cloth that is made expressly for the slaves. The dresses assumed by the negro minstrels, when they give imitations of plantation character, are by no means exaggerated; they are, instead, weak and unable to come up to the original. There was every variety of hats, with every imaginable slouch; and there was every cut and style of coat and pantaloons, made with every conceivable ingenuity of misfit, and tossed on with a general appearance of perfect looseness that is perfectly indescribable, except to say that a Southern negro always looks as if he could shake his clothes off without taking his hands out of his pockets.

The women, true to the feminine instinct, had made, in almost every case, some attempt at finery. All wore gorgeous turbans, generally manufactured in an instant out of a gay-colored handkerchief by a sudden and graceful twist of the fingers; though there was occasionally a more elaborate turban, a turban complex and mysterious, got up with care, and ornamented with a few beads or bright bits of ribbon.

Their dresses were mostly coarse stuff, though there were some gaudy calicoes; a few had ear-rings, and one possessed the treasure of a string of yellow and blue beads. The little children were always better and more carefully dressed than the older ones, the parental pride coming out in the shape of a yellow cap pointed like a mitre, or a jacket with a strip of red broadcloth round the bottom. The children were of all sizes, the youngest being fifteen days old. The babies were generally good-natured; though when one would set up a yell, the complaint soon attacked the others, and a full chorus would be the result.

The slaves remained at the Race-course, some of them for more than a week, and all of them for four days before the sale. They were brought in thus early that buyers who desired to inspect them might enjoy that privilege, although none of them were sold at private sale. For these preliminary days their shed was constantly visited by speculators. The negroes were examined with as little consideration as if they had been brutes indeed; the buyers pulling their mouths open to see their teeth, pinching their limbs to find how muscular they were, walking them up and down to detect any signs of lameness, making them stoop and bend in different ways that they might be certain there was no concealed rupture or wound; and in addition to all this treatment, asking them scores of questions relative to their qualifications and accomplishments. All these humiliations were submitted to without a murmur, and in some instances with good-natured cheerfulness--where the slave liked the appearance of the proposed buyer, and fancied that he might prove a kind "Mas'r."

The following curiously sad scene is the type of a score of others that were there enacted:

"Elisha," chattel No. 5 in the catalogue, had taken a fancy to a benevolent-looking middle-aged gentleman, who was inspecting the stock, and thus used his powers of persuasion to induce the benevolent man to purchase him, with his wife, boy and girl, Molly, Israel and Sevanda, chattels Nos. 6, 7 and 8. The earnestness with which the poor fellow pressed his suit, knowing, as he did, that perhaps the happiness of his whole life depended on his success, was touching, and the arguments he used most pathetic. He made no appeal to the feelings of the buyers; he rested no hope on his charity and kindness, but only strove to show how well worth his dollars were the bone and blood he was entreating him to buy.

"Look at me, Mas'r; am prime rice planter; sho' you won't find a better man den me; no better on de whole plantation; not a bit old yet; do mo' work den ever; do carpenter work, too, little; better buy me, Mas'r; I'se be good sarvant, Mas'r. Molly, too, my wife, Sa, fus'rate rice hand; mos as good as me. Stan' out yer, Molly, and let the gen'lm'n see."

Molly advances, with her hands crossed on her bosom, and makes a quick short curtsy, and stands mute, looking appealingly in the benevolent man's face. But Elisha talks all the faster.

"Show mas'r yer arm, Molly--good arm dat, Mas'r--she do a heap of work mo' with dat arm yet. Let good Mas'r see yer teeth, Molly--see dat Mas'r, teeth all reg'lar, all good--she'm young gal yet. Come out yer, Israel, walk aroun' an' let the gen'lm'n see how spry you be"--

Then, pointing to the three-year-old girl who stood with her chubby hand to her mouth, holding on to her mother's dress, and uncertain what to make of the strange scene.

"Little Vardy's only a chile yet; make prime gal by-and-by. Better buy us, Mas'r, we'm fus' rate bargain"--and so on. But the benevolent gentleman found where he could drive a closer bargain, and so bought somebody else.

Similar scenes were transacting all the while on every side parents praising the strength and cleverness of their children, and showing off every muscle and sinew to the very best advantage, not with the excusable pride of other parents, but to make them the more desirable in the eyes of the man-buyer; and, on the other hand, children excusing and mitigating the age and inability of parents, that they might be more marketable and fall, if possible, into kind hands. Not unfrequently these representations, if borne out by the facts, secured a purchaser. The women never spoke to the white men unless spoken to, and then made the conference as short as possible. And not one of them all, during the whole time they were thus exposed to the rude questions of vulgar men, spoke the first unwomanly or indelicate word, or conducted herself in any regard otherwise than as a modest woman should do; their conversation and demeanor were quite as unexceptionable as they would have been had they been the highest ladies in the land, and through all the insults to which they were subjected they conducted themselves with the most perfect decorum and self-respect.

The sentiment of the subjoined characteristic dialogue was heard more than once repeated:

"Well, Colonel, I seen you looking sharp at Shoemaker Bill's Sally. Going to buy her?

"Well, Major, I think not. Sally's a good, big, strapping gal, and can do a heap o'work; but it's five years since she had any children. *She's done breeding, I reckon.*"

In the intervals of more active labor, the discussion of the re-opening of the slave trade was commenced, and the opinion seemed to generally prevail that its reestablishment is a consummation devoutly to be wished, and one red-faced Major or General or Corporal clenched his remarks with the emphatic assertion that "We'll have all the niggers in Africa over here in three years--we won't leave enough for seed."

THE SALE.

The Race-course at Savannah is situated about three miles from the city, in a pleasant spot, nearly surrounded by woods. As it rained violently during the two days of the sale, the place was only accessible by carriages, and the result was, that few attended but actual buyers, who had come from long distances, and could not afford to lose the opportunity. If the affair had come off in Yankee land, there would have been a dozen omnibuses running constantly between the city and the Race-course, and some speculator would have bagged a nice little sum of money by the operation. But nothing of the kind was thought of here, and the only gainers were the livery stables, the owners of which had sufficient Yankeeism to charge double and treble prices.

The conveniences for getting to the ground were so limited that there were not enough buyers to warrant the opening of the sale for an hour or two after the advertised time. They dropped in, however, a few at a time, and things began to look more encouragingly for the seller.

The negroes looked more uncomfortable than ever; the close confinement in-doors for a number of days, and the drizzly, unpleasant weather, began to tell on their condition. They moved about more listlessly, and were fast losing the activity and springiness they had at first shown. This morning they were all gathered into the long room of the building erected as the "Grand Stand" of the Race-course, that they might be immediately under the eye of the buyers. The room was about a hundred feet long by twenty wide, and herein were crowded the poor creatures, with much of their baggage, awaiting their respective calls to step upon the block and be sold to the highest bidder. This morning Mr. Pierce Butler appeared among his people, speaking to each one, and being recognized with seeming pleasure by all. The men obsequiously pulled off their hats and made that indescribable sliding hitch with the foot which passes with a negro for a bow; and the women each dropped the quick curtsy, which they seldom vouchsafe to any other than their legitimate master and mistress. Occasionally, to a very old or favorite servant, Mr. Butler would extend his gloved hand, which mark of condescension was instantly hailed with grins of delight from all the sable witnesses.

The room in which the sale actually took place immediately adjoined the room of the negroes, and communicated with it by two large doors. The sale room was open to the air on one side, commanding a view of the entire Course. A small platform was raised about two feet and a-half high, on which were placed the desks of the entry clerks, leaving room in front of them for the auctioneer and the goods.

At about 11 o'clock the business men took their places, and announced that the sale would begin. Mr. Bryan, the Negro Broker, is a dapper little man, wearing spectacles and a yachting hat, sharp and sudden in his movements, and perhaps the least bit in the world obtrusively officious--as earnest in his language as he could be without actual swearing, though acting much as if he would like to swear a little at the critical moment; Mr. Bryan did not sell the goods, he merely superintended the operation, and saw that the entry clerks did their duty properly.

The auctioneer proper was a Mr. Walsh, who deserves a word of description. In personal appearance he is the very opposite of Mr. Bryan, being careless in his dress instead of scrupulous, a large man instead of a little one, a fat man instead of a lean one, and a good-natured man instead of a fierce one. He is a rollicking old boy, with an eye ever on the look-out, and that never lets a bidding nod escape him; a hearty word for every bidder who cares for it, and plenty of jokes to let off when the business gets a little slack. Mr. Walsh has a florid complexion, not more so, perhaps, than is becoming, and possibly not more so than is natural in a whiskey country. Not only is his face red, but his skin has been taken off in spots by blisters of some sort, giving him a peely look; so that, taking his face all in all, the peeliness and the redness combined, he looks much as if he had been boiled in the same pot with a red cabbage.

Mr. Walsh mounted the stand and announced the terms of the sale, "one-third cash, the remainder payable in two equal annual instalments, bearing interest from the day of sale, to be secured by approved mortgage and personal security, or approved acceptances in Savannah, Ga., or Charleston, S. C. Purchasers to pay for papers."

The buyers, who were present to the number of about two hundred, clustered around the platform; while the negroes, who were not likely to be immediately wanted, gathered into sad groups in the back-ground, to watch the progress of the selling in which they were so sorrowfully interested. The wind howled outside, and through the open side of the building the driving rain came pouring in; the bar down stairs ceased for a short time its brisk trade; the buyers lit fresh cigars, got ready their catalogues and pencils, and the first lot of human chattels was led upon the stand, not by a white man, but by a sleek mulatto, himself a slave, and who seems to regard the selling of his brethren, in which he so glibly assists, as a capital joke. It had been announced that the negroes would be sold in "families," that is to say, a man would not be parted from his wife, or a mother from a very young child. There is perhaps as much policy as humanity in this arrangement, for thereby many aged and unserviceable people are disposed of, who otherwise would not find a ready sale.

The first family brought out were announced on the catalogue as

NAME	AGE.	REMARKS
1. George,	27 -------	Prime Cotton Planter.

2. Sue, 26-------- Prime Rice Planter.
3. George, - - 6 Boy Child.
4. Harry, - - - 2 Boy Child.

The manner of buying was announced to be bidding a certain price a-piece for the whole lot. Thus, George and his family were started at $300, and were finally sold at $600 each, being $2,400 for the hour. To get an idea of the relative value of each one, we must suppose George worth $1,200, Sue worth $900, Little George worth $200, and Harry worth $100. Owing, however, to some misapprehension on the part of the buyer, as to the manner of bidding, he did not take the family at this figure, and they were put up and sold again, on the second day, when they brought $620 each, or $2,480 for the whole--an advance of $80 over the first sale.

Robert, and Luna his wife, who were announced as having "goitre, otherwise very prime," brought the round sum of $1,005 each. But that your readers may have an idea of the exact manner in which things are done, I append a couple of pages of the catalogue used on this occasion, which you can print verbatim:

99-Kate's John, aged 31; rice, prime man.
100-Betsey, 20; rice, unsound.
101-Kate. 6
102-Violet, 3 months.
Sold for $510 each.

103-Wooster, 45; hand, and fair mason.
104--Mary, 40; cotton hand.
Sold for $300 each.

105--Commodore Bob, aged; rice hand.
106--Kate, aged; cotton.
107--Linda, 19; cotton, prime young woman.
108--Joe, 13; rice, prime boy.
Sold for $600 each.

109--Bob, 30; rice.
110--Mary, 25; rice, prime woman.
Sold for $1,135 each.

111--Anson, 49; rice,-ruptured, one eye.
112--Violet, 55; rice hand.

Sold for $250 each.

113--Allen Jeffrey, 46; rice hand and sawyer in steam mill.
114--Sikey, 43; rice hand.
115--Watty, 5; infirm legs.
Sold for $250 each.

116--Rina, 18; rice, prime young woman.
117--Lena, 1.
Sold for $645 each.

118--Pompey, 31; rice-lame in one foot.
119--Kitty, 30; rice, prime woman.
120--Pompey, Jr., 10; prime boy.
121--John, 7.
122--Noble, 1; boy.
Sold for $580 each.

341--Goin, 39; rice hand.
342--Cassander, 35; cotton hand-has fits.
343--Emiline, 19; cotton, prime young woman.
344--Judy, 11; cotton, prime girl.
Sold for $400 each.
345--Dorcas, 17; cotton, prime woman.
346--Joe, 3 months.
Sold for $1,200 each.

347--Tom, 22; cotton hand. Sold for $1,260.
348--Judge Will, 55; rice hand. Sold for $325.
349--Lowden, 54; cotton hand.
350--Hagar, 50; cotton hand.
351--Lowden, 15; cotton, prime boy.
352--Silas, 13; cotton, prime boy.
353--Lettia, 11; cotton, prime girl.
Sold for $300 each.

354--Fielding, 21; cotton, prime young man.
355--Abel, 19; cotton, prime young man.
Sold for $1,295 each.

356--Smith's Bill, aged; sore leg.
357--Leah, 46; cotton hand.
358--Sally, 9.
Withdrawn.

359--Adam, 24; rice, prime man.
360--Charlotte, 22; rice prime woman.
361--Lesh, 1.
Sold for $570 each.

362--Maria, 47; rice hand.
363--Luna, 22; rice, prime woman.
364--Clementina, 17; rice, prime young woman.

Sold for $950 each.

365--Tom, 48; rice hand.
366--Harriet, 41; rice hand
367--Wanney, 19; rice hand, prime young man.368-Deborah, 6.
369--Infant, 3 months.
Sold for $700 each.

It seems as if every shade of character capable of being implicated in the sale of human flesh and blood was represented among the buyers. There was the Georgia fast young man, with his pantaloons tucked into his boots, his velvet cap jauntily dragged over to one side, his cheek full of tobacco, which he bites from a huge plug, that resembles more than anything else an old bit of a rusty wagon tire, and who is altogether an animal of quite a different breed from your New York fast man. His ready revolver, or his convenient knife, is ready for instant use in case of heated argument. White-neck-clothed, gold-spectacled, and silver-haired old men were there, resembling in appearance that noxious breed of sanctimonious deacons we have at the North, who are perpetually leaving documents at your door that you never read, and the business of whose mendicant life it is to eternally solicit subscriptions for charitable associations, of which they are treasurers. These gentry, with quiet step and subdued voice, moved carefully about among the live stock, ignoring, as a general rule, the men, but tormenting the women with questions which, when accidentally overheard by the disinterested spectator, bred in that spectator's mind an almost irresistible desire to knock somebody down. And then, all imaginable varieties of rough, backwoods rowdies, who began the day in a spirited manner, but who, as its hours progressed, and their practice at the bar became more prolific in results, waxed louder and talkier and more violent, were present, and added a characteristic feature to the assemblage.

Those of your readers who have read "Uncle Tom,"--and who has not?--will remember, with peculiar feelings, Legree, the slave-driver and woman-whipper. That that character is not been overdrawn, or too highly colored, there is abundant testimony. Witness the subjoined dialogue: A party of men were conversing on the fruitful subject of managing refractory "niggers;" some were for severe whipping, some recommending branding, one or two advocated other modes of torture, but one huge brute of a man, who had not taken an active part in the discussion, save to assent, with approving nod, to any unusually barbarous proposition, at last broke his silence by saying, in an oracular way, "You may say what you like about managing niggers; I'm a driver myself, and I've had some experience, and I ought to know. You can manage ordinary niggers by lickin' 'em, and givin' 'em a taste of the hot iron once in awhile when they're extra ugly; but if a nigger really sets himself up against me, I can't never have any patience with him. I just get my pistol and shoot him right down; and that's the best way."

And this brute was talking to gentlemen, and his remarks were listened to with attention, and his assertions assented to by more than one in the knot of listeners. But all this time the sale was going on, and the merry Mr. Walsh, with many a quip and jest, was beguiling the time when the bidding was slow.

The expression on the faces of all who stepped on the block was always the same, and told of more anguish than it is in the power of words to express. Blighted homes, crushed hopes and broken hearts, was the sad story to be read in all the anxious faces. Some of them regarded the sale with perfect indifference, never making a motion, save to turn from one side to the other at the word of the dapper Mr. Bryan, that all the crowd might have a fair view of their proportions, and then, when the sale was accomplished, stepped down from the block without caring to cast even a look at the buyer, who now held all their happiness in his hands. Others, again, strained their eyes with eager glances from one buyer to another as the bidding went on, trying with earnest attention to follow the rapid voice of the auctioneer. Sometimes, two persons only would be bidding for the same chattel, all the others having resigned the contest, and then the poor creature on the block, conceiving an instantaneous preference for one of the buyers over the other, would regard the rivalry with the intensest interest, the expression of his face changing with every bid, settling into a half smile of joy if the favorite buyer persevered unto the end and secured the property, and settling down into a look of hopeless despair if the other won the victory.

DAPHNEY's BABY.

The family of Primus, plantation carpenter, consisting of Daphney his wife, with her young babe, and Dido, a girl of three years old, were reached in due course of time. Daphney had a large shawl, which she kept carefully wrapped round her infant and herself. This unusual proceeding attracted much attention, and provoked many remarks, such as these:

"What do you keep your nigger covered up for? Pull off her blanket."

"What's the matter with the gal? Has she got the headache?"

"What's the fault of the gal? Ain't she sound? Pull off her rags and let us see her."

"Who's going to bid on that nigger, if you keep her covered up. Let's see her face."

And a loud chorus of similar remarks, emphasized with profanity, and mingled with sayings too indecent and obscene to be even hinted at here, went up from the crowd of chivalrous Southern gentlemen.

At last the auctioneer obtained a hearing long enough to explain that there was no attempt to practise any deception in the case-the parties were not to be wronged in any way; he had no desire to palm off on them an inferior article; but the truth of the matter was that Daphney had been confined only fifteen days ago, and he thought that on that account she was entitled to the slight indulgence of a blanket, to keep from herself and child the chill air and the driving rain.

Will your lady readers look at the circumstances of this case?

The day was the 2d day of March. Daphney's baby was born into the world on St. Valentine's happy day, the 14th of February.

Since her confinement, Daphney had traveled from the plantation to Savannah, where she had been kept in a shed for six days. On the sixth or seventh day after her sickness, she had left her bed, taken a railroad journey across the country to the shambles, was there exposed for six days to the questionings and insults of the negro speculators, and then on the fifteenth day after he confinement was put on the block, with her husband and her other child, and, with her new-born baby in her arms, sold to the highest bidder.

It was very considerate of Daphney to be sick before the sale, for her wailing babe was worth to Mr. Butler all of a hundred dollars. The family sold for $625 a-piece, or $2,500 for the four.

BOB AND MARY.

This was a couple not quite a year married, and were down in the catalogue as "prime." They had no children yet; Mary, with a reprehensible lack of that tender interest in Mr. Butler's affairs that had been exibited in so eminent a degree by Daphney, had disappointed that worthy man's expectations, and the baby as yet was not. But Bob and Mary sold for $1,135 a-piece, for all that.

In another instance, Margaret, the wife of Doctor George, who was confined on February 16, though the name of herself and family were inserted in the catalogue, did not come to the sale, and consequently, they were not disposed of at all. As Margaret's baby was full four days old at the time she was required to start on her journey to Savannah, we can only look at her refusal to go as a most culpable, instance of perversity.

Margaret should be whipped, and branded, and otherwise kindly admonished of her great sin in thus disappointing the reasonable expectations of so kind a master. But Mr. Butler bore with her in a truly Christian spirit, and uttered no reproach--in public at least. It was the more unkind of

Margaret, too, because there were six in the family who would have brought probably $4,000, and all were detained form the sale by the contumacy of misguided Margaret.

While on the subject of babies, it may be mentioned that Amity, chattel No. 316, wife of Prince, chattel No. 315, had testified her earnest desire to contribute all in her power to the worldly wealth of her master by bringing into the world at one time chattles Nos. 317 and 318, be being a fine pair of twin boys, just a year old. It is not in the evidence that Amity received from her master any testimonial of his appreciating her good behavior on this occasion, but it is certain that she brought a great price, the four, Prince, Amity and the twins selling for $670 a-piece, being a total of $2,680.

Many other babies, of all ages of baby-hood, were sold, but there was nothing particularly interesting about them. There were some thirty babies in the lot; they are esteemed worth to the master a hundred dollars the day they are born, and to increase in value at the rate of a hundred dollars a year till they are sixteen or seventeen years old, at which age they bring the best prices.

THE LOVE STORY OF JEFFREY AND DORCAS.

Jeffrey, chattel No. 319, marked as a "prime cotton hand," aged 23 years, was put up. Jeffrey being a likely lad, the competition was high. The first bid was $1,100, and he was finally sold for $1,310. Jeffrey was sold alone; he had no incumbrance in the shape of an aged father or mother, who must necessarily be sold with him; nor had he any children, for Jeffrey was not married. But Jeffrey, chattel No. 319, being human in his affections, had dared to cherish a love for Dorcas, chattel No. 278; and Dorcas, not having the fear of her master before her eyes, had given her heart to Jeffrey. Whether what followed was a just retribution on Jeffrey and Dorcas, for daring to take such liberties with their master's property as to exchange hearts, or whether it only goes to prove that with black as with white the saying holds, that "the course of true love never did run smooth," cannot now be told. Certain it is that these two lovers were not to realize to consummation of their hopes in happy wedlock.

Jeffrey and Dorcas had told their loves, had exchanged their simple vows, and were betrothed, each to the other as dear, and each by the other as fondly beloved as though their skins had been of fairer color. And who shall say that, in the sight of Heaven and all holy angels, these two humble hearts were not as closely wedded as any two of the prouder race that call them slaves?

Be that as it may, Jeffrey was sold. He finds out his new-master; and' hat in hand, the big tears standing in his eyes, and his voice t trembling with emotion, he stands before that master and tells his simple story, praying that his betrothed may be bought with him. Though his voice trembles, there is no embarrassment in his manner; his fears have killed all the bashfulness that would naturally attend such a recital to a stranger, and before unsympathizing witnesses; he feels that he is pleading for the happiness of her he loves, as well as for his own, and his tale is told in a frank and manly way.

"I loves Dorcas, young Mas'r; I loves her well an' true; she says she loves me, and I know she does; de good Lord knows I loves her better than I loves any one in de wide world--never can love another woman half as well. Please buy Dorcas, Mas'r. We're be good sarvants to you long as we live. We're be married right soon, young Mas'r, and de chillun will be healthy and strong, Mas'r, and dey'll be good sarvants, too. Please buy Dorcas, young Mas'r. We loves each other a heap--do, really true, Mas'r."

Jeffrey then remembers that no loves and hopes of his are to enter into the bargain at all, but in the earnestness of his love he has forgotten to base his plea on other ground till now, when he bethinks him and continues, with his voice not trembling now, save with eagerness to prove how worthy of many dollars is the maiden of his heart:

"Young Mas'r, Dorcas prime woman--A1 woman, sa. Tall gal, sir; long arms, strong, healthy, and can do a heap of work in a day. She is one of de best rice hands on de whole plantation; worth $1,200 easy, Mas'r, an' fus'rate bargain at that."

The man seems touched by Jeffrey's last remarks, and bids him fetch out his "gal, and let's see what she looks like."

Jeffrey goes into the long room, and presently returns with Dorcas, looking very sad and self-possessed, without a particle of embarrassment at the trying position in which she is placed. She makes the accustomed curtsy, and stands meekly with her hands clasped across her bosom, waiting the result. The buyer regards her with a critical eye, and growls in a low voice that the "gal has good p'ints." Then he goes on to a more minute and careful examination of her working abilities. He turns her around, makes her stoop, and walk; and then he takes off her turban to look at her head that no wound or disease be concealed by the gay handkerchief; he looks at her teeth, and feels of her arms, and at last announces himself pleased with the result of his observations, whereat Jeffrey, who has stood near, trembling with eager hope, is overjoyed, and he smiles for the first time. The buyer then crowns Jeffrey's happiness by making a promise that he will buy her, if the price isn't run up too high. And the two lovers step aside and congratulate each other on their good fortune. But Dorcas is not to be sold till the next day, and there are twenty-four long hours of feverish expectation.

Early next morning is Jeffrey alert, and, hat in hand, encouraged to unusual freedom by the greatness of the stake for which he plays, he addresses every buyer, and of all who will listen he begs the boon of a word to be spoken to his new master to encourage him to buy Dorcas. And all the long morning he speaks in his homely way with all who know him, that they will intercede to save his sweetheart from being sold away from him forever. No one has the heart to deny a word of promise and encouragement to the poor fellow, and, joyous with so much kindness, his hopes and spirits gradually rise until he feels almost certain that the wish of heart will be accomplished. And Dorcas, too, is smiling, for is not Jeffrey's happiness her own?

At last comes the trying moment, and Dorcas steps up on the stand.

But now a most unexpected feature in the drama is for the first time unmasked: *Dorcas is not to be sold alone*, but with a family of four others. Full of dismay, Jeffrey looks to his master, who shakes his head, for, although he might be induced to buy Dorcas alone, he has no use for the rest of the family. Jeffrey reads his doom in his master's look, and turns away, the tears streaming down his honest face.

So Dorcas is sold, and her toiling life is to be spent in the cotton fields of South Carolina, while Jeffrey goes to the rice plantation of the Great Swamp.

And to-morrow, Jeffrey and Dorcas are to say their tearful fare-well, and go their separate ways in life, to meet no more as mortal beings.

But didn't Mr. Pierce Butler give them a silver dollar a-piece? Who shall say there is no magnanimity in slave-owners?

In another hour I see Dorcas in the long room, sitting motionless as a statute, with her head covered with a shawl. And I see Jeffrey, who goes to his new master, pulls off his hat and says: "I'se very much obliged, Mas'r, to you for tryin' to help me. I knows you would have done it if you could--thank you, Mas'r--thank you--but--its--berry--hard"--and hear the poor fellow breaks down entirely and walks away, covering his face with his battered hat, and sobbing like a very child.

He is soon surrounded by a group of his colored friends, who, with an instinctive delicacy most unlooked for, stand quiet, and with uncovered heads, about him.

Anson and Violet, chattels Nos. 111 and 112, were sold for $250 each, both being old, and Anson being down in the catalogue as "ruptured and as having one eye." Violet was sold as being sick. Her disease was probably consumption, which supposition gave rise to the following feeling conversation between two buyers:

"Cheap gal, that, Major!"

"Don't think so. They may talk about her being sick; it's no easy sickness see's got. She's got consumption, and the man that buys her 'll have to be a doctrin' her all the time, and she'll die in less than three months. I won't have anything to do with her--don't want any half dead niggers about me."

THE MARKET VALUE OF AN EYE.

Guy, chattel No. 419, "a prime young man," sold for $1,280, being without blemish; his age was twenty years, and he was altogether a fine article. His next-door neighbor, Andrew, chattel No. 420, was very counterpart in all marketable points, in size, age, skill, and everything save that he had lost his right eye. Andrew sold for only $1,040, from which we argue that the market value of the right eye in the Southern country is

$240.

AN UNEXPECTED MARRIAGE.

When the family of Mingo, consisting of his wife, two sons and a daughter, was called for, it was announced by the auctioneer that chattel No. 322, Dembo, the eldest son, aged 20, had the evening before procured the services of a minister, and been joined in wedlock to chattel No. 404, Frances, and that he should be compelled to put up the bride and groom in one lot. They were called up, and, as was to be expected, their appearance was the signal for a volley of coarse jokes from the auctioneer, and of ribald remarks from the surrounding crowd. The newly-married pair bore it bravely, although one refined gentleman took hold of Frances's lips and pulled them apart, to see her age.

This sort of thing it is that makes Northern blood boil, and Northern fists clench with a luadable desire to hit somebody. It was almost too much for endurance to stand and see those brutal slave-drivers pushing the women about, pulling their lips apart with their not too cleanly hands, and committing many another indecent act, while the husbands, fathers and brothers of those women were compelled to witness these things, without the power to resent the outrage.

Dembo and Frances were at last struck off for $1,320 each, and went to spend their honey-moon on a cotton plantation in Alabama.

THE CASE OF JOSHUA's MOLLY.

The auctioneer brought up Joshua's Molly and family. He announced that Molly insisted that she was lame in her left foot, and perversely would walk lame, although for his part, he did not believe a word of it. He had caused her to be examined by an eminent physician in Savannah, which medical light had declared that Joshua's Molly was not lame, but was only shamming. However, the gentlemen must judge for themselves and bid accordingly. So Molly was put through her paces, and compelled to trot up and down along the stage, to go up and down the steps, and to exercise her feet in various ways, but always with the same result, the left foot *would* be lame. She was finally sold for $695.

Whether she really was lame or not no one knows but herself, but it must be remembered that to a slave a lameness, or anything that decreases his market value, is a thing to be rejoiced over. A man in the prime of life, worth $1,600 or thereabouts, can have little hope of ever being able, by any little savings of his own, to purchase his liberty. But let him have a rupture, or lose a limb, or sustain any other injury that renders him of much less service to his owner, and reduces his value to $300 or $400, and he may hope to accumulate that sum, and eventually to purchase his liberty. Freedom without health is infinitely sweeter than health without freedom.

And so the Great Sale went on for two long days, during which time there were sold 429 men, women and children. There were 436 announced to be sold, but a few were detained on the plantations by sickness.

At the close of the sale, on the last day, several baskets of champagne were produced, and all were invited to partake, the wine being at the expense of the broker, Mr. Bryan.

The total amount of the sale foots up $303,850--the proceeds of the first day being $161,480, and of the second day $142,370.

The highest sum paid for any one family was given for Sally Walker and her five children, who were mostly grown up. The price was $6,180.

The highest price paid for a single man was $1,750, which was given for William, a "fair carpenter and caulker."

The highest price paid for a woman was $1,250, which was given for Jane, "cotton hand and house servant."

The lowest price paid was for Anson and Violet, a gray-haired couple, each having numbered more than fifty years; they brought but $250 a piece.

MR. PIERCE BUTLER GIVES HIS PEOPLE A DOLLAR A-PIECE.

Leaving the Race buildings, where the scenes we have described took place, a crowd of negroes were seen gathered eagerly about a white man. That man was Pierce M. Butler, of the free City of Philadelphia, who was solacing the wounded hearts of the people he had sold from their firesides and their homes, by doling out to them small change at the rate of a dollar a head. To every negro he had sold, who presented his claim for the paltry pittance, he gave the munificent stipend of one whole dollar, in specie; he being provided with two canvas bags of 25 cent pieces, fresh from the mint, to give an additional glitter to his generosity.

And now come the scenes of the last partings--of the final separations of those who were akin, or who had been such dear friends from youth that no ties of kindred could bind them closer--of those who were all in all to each other, and for whose bleeding hearts there shall be no earthly comfort--the parting of parents and children, of brother from brother, and the rending of sister from a sister's bosom; and O! hardest, cruellest of all, the tearing asunder of loving hearts, wedded in all save the one ceremony of the Church-these scenes pass all description; it is not meet for pen to meddle with tears so holy.

As the last family stepped down the block, the rain ceased, for the first time in four days the clouds broke away, and the soft sunlight fell on the scene. The unhappy slaves had many of them been already removed, and others were now departing with their new masters.

That night, not a steamer left that Southern port, not a train of cars sped away from that cruel city. that did not bear each its own sad burden of those unhappy ones, whose only crime is that they are not strong and wise. Some of them maimed and wounded, some scarred and gashed, by accident, or by the hand of ruthless drivers--all sad and sorrowful as human hearts can be.

But the stars shone out as brightly as if such things had never been, the blushing fruit-trees poured their fragrance on the evening air, and the scene was an calmly sweet and quiet as if Man had never marred the glorious beauties of Earth by deeds of cruelty and wrong.

www.ingramcontent.com/pod-product-compliance
Ingram Content Group UK Ltd.
Pitfield, Milton Keynes, MK11 3LW, UK
UKHW041838200726
13854UKWH00003BA/1210